CW00895032

just

THE JOB

Teaching

*Also published in the **Just the Job!** series:*

just THE JOB

Teaching

Lifetime Careers
WILTSHIRE

Hodder & Stoughton

A MEMBER OF THE HODDER HEADLINE GROUP

Just the Job! draws directly on the CLIPS careers information database developed and maintained by Lifetime Careers Wiltshire and used by almost every careers service in the UK. The database is revised annually using a rigorous update schedule and incorporates material collated through desk/telephone research and information provided by all the professional bodies, institutions and training bodies with responsibility for course accreditation and promotion of each career area.

ISBN 0 340 68774 6
First published 1997

Impression number	10	9	8	7	6	5	4	3	2	1
Year	2002	2001	2000	1999	1998	1997				

Printed in Great Britain for Hodder & Stoughton Educational, the educational publishing division of Hodder Headline Plc, 338 Euston Road, London NW1 3BH, by Cox & Wyman Ltd, Reading, Berkshire.

just
THE
JOB

CONTENTS

support assistant. Escort on school transport. Matron
and assistant matron. Midday supervisory assistant.
School meals service. School crossing patrol.
Laboratory assistant/technician. Information
technology coordinator/computer technician. Audio-
visual technician/resources technician. Grounds staff.
Caretaker. Cleaner.

Teacher trainers, educational advisers and inspectors.
Special projects. Education officer posts. Educational
administration. Additional specialisms. Teaching in
other situations. Other posts which may make use of
teachers' skills.

Working as a training officer in industry and commerce.
Independent training work. Instructors and trainers.

JUST THE JOB!

The *Just the Job!* series ranges over the entire spectrum of occupations and is intended to generate job ideas and stretch horizons of interest and possibility, allowing you to explore families of jobs for which you might have appropriate ability and aptitude. Each *Just the Job!* book looks in detail at a popular area or type of work, covering:

■ ways into work;
■ essential qualifications;
■ educational and training options;
■ working conditions;
■ progression routes;
■ potential career portfolios.

The information given in *Just the Job!* books is detailed and carefully researched. Obvious bias is excluded to give an even-handed picture of the opportunities available, and course details and entry requirements are positively checked in an annual update cycle by a team of careers information specialists. The text is written in approachable, plain English, with a minimum of technical terms.

In Britain today, there is no longer the expectation of a career for life, but support has increased for life-long learning and the acquisition of skills which will help young and old to make sideways career moves – perhaps several times during a working life – as well as moving into work carrying higher levels of responsibility and reward. *Just the Job!* invites you to select an appropriate direction for your *own* career progression.

Educational and vocational qualifications

A level – Advanced level of the General Certificate of Education

AS level – Advanced Supplementary level of the General Certificate of Education (equivalent to half an A level)

BTEC – Business and Technology Education Council: awards qualifications such as BTEC First, BTEC National Certificate/Diploma, etc

GCSE – General Certificate of Secondary Education

GNVQ/GSVQs – General National Vocational Qualification/ General Scottish Vocational Qualification: awarded at Foundation, Intermediate and Advanced levels by BTEC, City & Guilds of London Institute, Royal Society of Arts and SCOTVEC

HND/C – BTEC Higher National Diploma/Certificate

International Baccalaureate – recognised by all UK universities as equivalent to a minimum of two A levels

NVQ/SVQs – National/Scottish Vocational Qualifications: awarded by the National Council for Vocational Qualifications and the Scottish Vocational Education Council

PGCE – Postgraduate Certificate in Education

SCE – Scottish Certificate of Education, at **Standard** Grade (equate directly with GCSEs: grades 1–3 in SCEs at Standard Grade are equivalent to GCSE grades A–C) and **Higher** Grade (equate with the academic level attained after one year of a two-year A level course: three to five Higher Grades are broadly equivalent to two to four A levels at grades A–E)

Vocational work–based credits	NVQ/SVQ level 1	NVQ/SVQ level 2	NVQ/SVQ level 3	NVQ/SVQ level 4
Vocational qualifications: *a mix of theory and practice*	Foundation GNVQ/ GSVQ; BTEC First	Intermediate GNVQ/GSVQ	Advanced GNVQ/GSVQ; BTEC National Diploma/Certificate	BTEC Higher National Diploma/ Certificate
Educational qualifications	GCSE/SCE Standard Grade pass grades	GCSE grades A–C; SCE Standard Grade levels 1–3	Two A levels; four Scottish Highers; Baccalaureate	University degree

INTRODUCTION

Do you want to work with children and young people? Are you interested in their learning and development? Are you prepared for a demanding but rewarding career? Schools and colleges employ thousands of teachers as well as non-teaching staff. For teaching you will generally need to have gained a degree, but there are other jobs in schools where higher education qualifications are not required.

Through a career in teaching, you can make a personal input to the future of our society by working at first hand with children and young people, assisting them to develop their full potential. It is certainly a demanding occupation for which you will need plenty of stamina and enthusiasm. Some days can seem long and tiring, but others bring the intense satisfaction of assisting your students in acquiring new skills, and in developing logical thinking processes.

There is room in the profession for teachers to be individuals, just so long as you:

■ enjoy close contact with young people;
■ are enthusiastic about your specialist subject or subjects;
■ are well-organised and methodical in your approach to work.

There are opportunities for creativity, for the development of new methods of delivering subject matter, and training days in termtime through which to keep up to date with new approaches to teaching practice and classroom management.

Schools and colleges in England, Wales and Northern Ireland require their teaching staff to have a degree-level qualification and to have undergone formal teacher training to have achieved Qualified Teacher Status. There is no legal requirement for teachers in *independent* schools to have completed a period of teacher training, but many public and private schools do insist on applicants being formally qualified and, often, on being capable of teaching more than one subject. The system for training as a teacher is different in Scotland, and you should write to the TEACH centre in Edinburgh (see Further Information section) for full details.

If you enjoy working with children, there are other jobs in schools where higher education qualifications are not required. For example, you can work as a classroom assistant or specialist teaching assistant, helping the classroom teacher. These opportunities arise mainly at primary school level where teachers need extra help for their young readers, writers and mathematicians. For other opportunities to work with children, see *Care & Community* in the *Just the Job!* series.

TEACHING

Teachers train to teach children within particular age ranges: nursery (from three years), infants, juniors, or secondary (to sixteen or eighteen). Teaching three-year-olds obviously requires a very different approach to teaching ten-year-olds. Generally, in schools for children under eleven, teachers spend most of their time with a particular group of children teaching them *all* subjects – arithmetic, reading and writing, games, craft and so on. Nowadays, intending teachers have to obtain a degree-level qualification.

Most people think that they know what teachers do, because they have been at the receiving end of teaching for many years. But if you ask teachers what their work involves, their answers may be a bit different! Entry into teaching is now only for graduates – other than a few opportunities through the Licensed Teacher Scheme.

There is a lot more to teaching than working with pupils in the classroom. Outside lesson time there are many tasks which need to be tackled in a methodical and organised way. For instance:

- The year's work has to be planned so that all important topics are covered.
- Individual lessons have to be prepared and pupils' work marked – often in the evenings and at weekends.
- Assignments, tasks and tests are set and marked continually to assess pupils' progress.

- Records of the progress of each pupil must be kept, to see whether extra help or encouragement is needed.
- Annual reports have to be written.
- There are meetings to attend, often after school or in the evenings, to discuss matters with members of staff, or to meet parents.
- You have to keep yourself informed about new thinking and new methods of teaching your subject(s), and be flexible enough to adopt new ideas and put them into practice.
- In secondary schools, work experience programmes are planned and preparatory work done with pupils.

In the classroom, the teacher wants to get certain ideas across to pupils during a lesson. He or she must have imagination and confidence to stimulate and encourage quiet or lazy children to contribute, and stop unruly ones from disrupting other pupils. Keen, outgoing pupils must be encouraged, but not allowed to dominate the lesson.

The job varies according to which age group you work with. Teachers in secondary or further education usually teach one or two subjects only. They also have a role in caring for the personal and social development of a group of students, besides teaching their main subject.

Teachers of younger age groups, or children with special needs, are concerned with developing the full ability of individuals in *all* subjects, and work with the same group of children most of each day and throughout a whole academic year.

Would I like it?
- You need to be able to write and speak well.
- An interest in a specialist subject such as history, science, English, music or foreign languages will be useful.
- You will probably enjoy finding out about things and people.

- You will have an interest in working or dealing with all sorts of people.
- You will need to work under pressure.
- Some of the work is physically tiring, with long periods of standing.
- You may have to work at weekends or in the evenings.

Training to teach

Teachers in state schools undergo approved teacher training leading to Qualified Teacher Status (QTS). Usually you train to teach pupils within a specific age range – nursery, infant, primary, junior, junior/secondary, middle school and secondary.

In England and Wales, once you are qualified you are eligible to teach any age range, despite being trained for a limited age group only – though a complete change would be difficult and unusual. You can also train to teach in further education colleges, but, should you wish to transfer, an FE postgraduate teaching qualification is not acceptable for school teaching without further training. In Scotland, it is necessary to be qualified specifically for the age range you teach.

ENTRY QUALIFICATIONS

Teaching in state schools is now, for new entrants, generally an all-graduate profession, so you must have a degree. The degree could be a BEd (Bachelor of Education) or a degree in some other subject together with a postgraduate teaching qualification (PGCE). The only possible exception to this is the Licensed Teacher Scheme.

School/college-leavers

To get on to a degree course as a school/college-leaver normally requires:

- a minimum of two A levels (or the equivalent);

- supporting GCSEs which must include English and maths (grades A–C);
- for students born on or after 1 September 1979, a GCSE in a science subject at grade C will be required for entry for primary teacher training from September 1998.

Some potential PE, dance, drama and music teachers may be accepted for training with one A level, if they offer an extremely high standard in their practical subject.

Advanced GNVQs are suitable for entry to Higher Education. However, evidence of the content of the course being relevant to the school curriculum is required. GNVQ students may therefore be asked for an additional A level in a national curriculum subject.

The degree course entry requirements mentioned above may be relaxed for some mature entrants, whose applications are considered on individual merit. Adults with few or no qualifications wanting to train for teaching could consider following an Access course (minimum age varies between 21 and 24 years). As training for primary teaching may require you to specify a subject specialism, admissions tutors will often look for relevant school subjects in your A levels or Access course.

The Bachelor of Education (BEd) route
The BEd (or sometimes BSc or BA with QTS) is a combined degree and teacher training course, which lets you pursue academic study of one or more subjects from a wide range, whilst also studying the theory and practice of teaching. You can take a BEd at colleges of higher education and at universities.

Most courses run for four years, although there is now an increasing number of three-year BEd courses, and this trend will continue over the next few years. You need the minimum qualifications given above for entry. You can train for any age

range, but this route tends to be regarded as most suitable for nursery, primary and the lower years of secondary rather than for sixth form and other exam-oriented teaching. Secondary BEds are available mainly in business studies, craft, design technology, home economics, mathematics, physical education, physical sciences and religious education.

If you wish to enter initial teacher training and have satisfactorily completed the equivalent of one or two years of higher education – on the basis of qualifications, or through accreditation of prior learning – you can follow a shortened two-year BEd course. For example, two-year courses are offered in

15

subjects such as business studies, maths, science and technology for holders of BTEC Higher National or equivalent qualifications, who have commercial or industrial experience. Art training centres offer specialist courses to meet the needs of holders of approved qualifications in art and design.

A degree followed by a postgraduate teacher training course (PGCE)

If you take a degree at a university or other college, you can follow this with a one-year teacher training course leading to a Postgraduate Certificate in Education (PGCE). There are also a few two-year PGCE courses which offer subject conversion as well as teacher training, and some part-time courses. The Open University now offers a part-time distance learning PGCE which takes eighteen months: students can specialise in primary teaching of pupils aged 3–5/8 or 7–11 years, or in one of seven secondary subjects.

Your degree normally needs to be in a subject taught in schools and colleges, or to have included a large amount of subject matter relevant to curricular work – for instance, English, geography, languages, mathematics, sciences. Degrees in subjects like psychology (except for intending educational psychologists), law or town planning are not recommended. Subjects like astrophysics, engineering or biochemistry might be acceptable, however, since large amounts of basic mathematics or science would have been covered in the course. For primary education, candidates for teacher training should hold a UK degree (or a recognised equivalent), and the content of an entrant's previous education must provide the necessary foundation for work as a primary teacher.

To train by this route, you will need the minimum qualifications for entry. This route is generally thought to be the most suitable for those who wish to teach academic subjects to examination level in secondary education. Your degree needs to be appropriate to the school curriculum: check specific requirements with individual institutions. This study route has the advantages of delaying the need to make a firm commitment to teaching and of keeping open other career options. Note that there is keen competition for places on postgraduate courses for applicants with degrees in subjects such as history and social sciences. However, the government is currently seeking to promote increased recruitment to business studies, mathematics, science (particularly physics, chemistry and integrated science), PE, religious education and technology.

Other routes into teaching

Special two-year shortened BEd courses are offered to mature people wishing to train to teach certain subjects, such as maths, physics, chemistry, balanced science, design technology and information technology, modern languages, Welsh and religious education. Applicants need to have suitable professional or technical qualifications, and commercial or industrial experience.

The government is making money available to teacher-training providers for funding higher education recruitment of candidates on to one-year and two-year secondary courses in the priority subject areas mentioned above, or for enhancing the training provision in these areas.

The Licensed Teacher Scheme allows a relatively small number of unqualified people to enter teaching and gain their training on-the-job, over a two-year period. Applicants must be at least 24 years old, and need to have studied successfully for at least two years full-time at higher education level. The same English and maths GCSE requirements apply. Applications are made through the Teacher Training Agency. Places are extremely limited and graduates are generally preferred.

School–centred initial teacher training courses (SCITT) have recently been introduced in a limited number of school consortia and City Technology Colleges. The scheme aims to encourage postgraduate entry to teaching of those whose first degree is relevant to the school curriculum, and leads to Qualified Teacher Status. Where a higher education institute is involved in training, a PGCE may be awarded. Students are eligible for flat–rate, non–means–tested bursaries instead of the usual grants and loans. Details of this method of entry to teaching can be obtained from the Teacher Training Agency.

What teacher training involves

Whichever route you follow, the professional training involves similar components, though these are more intensive on a PGCE course than on a BEd, where there is more time.

All courses have now increased the amount of time spent in schools, to raise the level of trainee teachers' classroom practice. The theoretical part of training covers:

- the study of philosophy of education;
- the psychology of learning and communication;
- sociology (e.g. the effect of the home and the community on the learning potential of children);
- the history of education (e.g. how the present educational system has evolved).

Practical training involves observing experienced teachers at work and then taking control of classes yourself, to gain experience. You learn to prepare lessons; the techniques of communication; organisation and management of the class; methods of assessing pupils' work, and the effectiveness of your teaching. You are assigned to a school for several weeks at a time, during which **teaching practice** period your tutor visits you, to assess your progress. Some institutions offer short taster courses for people who think they might want to train in shortage subjects.

PROSPECTS

For experienced and qualified teachers there are opportunities for promotion up to the level of deputy or headteacher. Increments are paid to other teachers for extra pastoral or management responsibilities. In-service training is usually available to gain additional expertise or qualifications. There are limited opportunities as advisers and inspectors of schools, and lecturers on teacher training courses. Other possibilities include teaching abroad; working as an education officer for a museum, a field centre or a charity; working on a special research project; publishing, etc (see section on 'Opportunities outside teaching for trained teachers').

Teaching in nursery, infant and primary schools

Teaching young children is a very responsible and important job. The teacher gives the children ideas about school and learning which will remain with them for the rest of their school career and, possibly, for life. It is demanding work, which can be very tiring, but can also be extremely rewarding. Young children constantly ask questions, show you what they have done and need your help, praise and encouragement. There are various age ranges in which you can specialise when training, e.g. three to seven, five to eleven, eight to thirteen.

Virtually all new entrants to teaching are graduates. The **specialist teaching assistants**, or STAs, who assist teachers in the areas of reading, writing and mathematics in some primary schools, do not need formal qualifications above GCSE level (see later section).

Learning through doing

In teaching the youngest ('early years') children, the emphasis is very much on learning through playing, experiencing and doing. The teacher is as much concerned with developing children's language abilities and social skills as with more formal things like the beginnings of reading, writing, arithmetic, science and other subjects in the national curriculum.

Older primary children, who have gained the skills and concentration to do more sustained work, may require a somewhat different approach. In all cases, the teacher aims to provide challenges and experiences to develop and expand the child's curiosity and knowledge.

Planning, flexibility and sometimes being mum or dad
Good teachers organise their day carefully, planning what they want particular children to practise or experience. The children in a class spend a lot of the time working in small groups, or individually, on different activities, so teachers must be very well organised.

Yet teachers of young children can't be inflexible, or they would miss opportunities for learning. If workers are digging a hole in the road outside the classroom, the teacher is wiser to let the children learn about roads and noise, than to try to ignore it! The day is more flexible than in a secondary school – bells don't ring every 45 minutes.

Generally, teachers of young children make a lot of their own teaching materials. All this has to be fitted in with assessment, and evaluation of each child's progress.

With nursery-age children and infants, the teacher often has to be a part-time parent, helping them with shoelaces, tending minor ills and sorting out their problems. Nursery schools and some infant schools have **nursery nurses** to help, but they are rather rare in infant/primary schools! Working with three-year-olds in a nursery school will involve assisting with very basic aspects of the children's development – including speech and physical coordination.

The teacher in a nursery, infant or primary school usually

spends most of his or her time with the same group of children. This means a good relationship can be built up, but it also produces its own stresses, because small children are very demanding. In some schools, two teachers may share responsibility for a larger group of children, to allow for flexibility in activities. Classrooms may be 'open-plan', with furniture and carpeting separating areas for different types of work.

There may be specialists for some 'subjects', such as physical education, music, mathematics, etc.

Schools

Schools vary enormously in size, from those with less than thirty children in some villages, to city schools with over 600. The size of the school affects the day-to-day job. In a small school of around sixty children, there would typically be three teachers and small, mixed-age classes – one for infants up to about seven, one for lower juniors up to nine, and one for top juniors up to eleven. By comparison, a larger school may have one or two teachers for each year and classes of over thirty children.

In bigger schools, there are more opportunities for teachers to take on special responsibility for areas such as language, mathematics or music, and the higher paid 'special responsibility' posts.

What it takes

Teachers of young children need a wide range of abilities, interests and skills. Some of these attributes may be developed during training; others may already be held.

- Music, art and craft skills are always welcome.
- Interests like physical education and drama are also valued.
- Sound health is important. The job is physically demanding and teachers are exposed to all sorts of colds and stomach upsets in schools. A teacher who is frequently off sick is a liability!

However, do note that some people with disabilities have successfully made careers in teaching; if you have a disability, you would need to make careful enquiries before applying for a training course.

John – a primary school teacher

❝ It's hard to describe the real buzz I get when a child learns to do something simple that he or she couldn't do before, whether it's tying up their shoelaces or understanding how to add up. That's what keeps me going. I love being around small children as they're so interesting and rewarding. If I can encourage them to enjoy learning at this age, then they're off to a pretty good start.

I chose to work in a small school, where I teach children from five to eight years old. It is an extremely demanding job, as the children, especially the younger ones, are always asking for attention or for a bit of reassurance. They can't concentrate for very long. With fairly large classes, it's really difficult to give each child your individual attention, but I try to be methodical about it and make sure no one is neglected. I'm not always as patient as I would like to be, but I do have a good laugh every now and then.

The job doesn't begin and end in the classroom. I have to be in school before 8.00 a.m. for playground duty and work on after school ends till around 6.00 p.m., as there are lessons to prepare, meetings to attend, reading to do (to keep up to date with all the changes) and extra-curricular activities to arrange. At the moment I'm organising a nature trail around the local National Trust land, which should be interesting.

I have a physics degree, plus a postgraduate teaching qualification, which meant I was in great demand, although, working with this age group, I teach a wide range of subjects. My next step is to become a deputy head, but that's some way in the future. ❞

ROUTES TO QUALIFYING AS A PRIMARY TEACHER

The main route into primary level teaching is through the Bachelor of Education (BEd) degree. There are a few Postgraduate Certificate in Education (PGCE) courses which train would-be primary teachers, but competition for places is fierce. On a BEd course, you will study a primary level national curriculum subject to degree level as well as train to teach across all subjects of the primary curriculum. An alternative is the new six-subject BEd for primary teaching which is being introduced. For the PGCE route, your previous education should provide the 'necessary foundation for work as a primary school teacher'. Institutions will advise on their own specific entry requirements.

Independent training

There are also the independent education training systems, most of which follow a particular, sometimes individual, philosophical approach to the education of very young children. For example, there are Rudolf Steiner schools which train their own staff to encourage child development and learning in line with Steiner's beliefs. Montessori training establishments are based on Dr Montessori's ideas of freedom for the child to learn in a carefully planned environment. Training to teach by one of these systems is unacceptable on its own for the state school system, and leads rather to jobs in privately-run nurseries, nursery and junior schools. You are unlikely to get a grant for these courses, but as they are shorter than normal teaching courses (one or two academic years), it may be feasible to finance them independently. Some Montessori training centres offer part-time and distance learning courses.

PROSPECTS

Full-time and part-time jobs are reasonably easy to find, and there is concern over a growing shortage of primary teachers in the next decade. Prospects are best for infant and junior teachers: nursery school provision is patchy, although nursery schools and playgroups are receiving official encouragement at present and the level of provision may well expand. Many nursery schools are privately run, and starting up a nursery is an option which may appeal to those with sufficient capital. In the primary sector, church-controlled schools are common and they may require staff (especially headteachers) to be practising members of the appropriate religion.

Teaching in secondary schools

Unlike teachers in primary schools, secondary teachers are usually specialists in particular subjects. Most new entrants have taken a degree in their subject of interest, followed by a postgraduate teaching qualification, or they have specialised in the subject during their Bachelor of Education (BEd) degree course.

The subjects that you can train to teach are largely dictated by the national curriculum and by the A levels that you take. Job opportunities in teaching will depend on the subjects you can offer an employer.

In general, the subject areas with the greatest shortage of suitable applicants are (in alphabetical order) business studies, chemistry, design and information technology, mathematics, modern languages, music, physics and religious education. Arts, classics, humanities, biology and physical education posts are less hard to fill. However, shortages of teachers in nearly every secondary school subject have been predicted over the next few years.

There are also various specialisations within secondary school work into which experienced teachers can move after some in-service training to gain additional expertise or qualifications. For instance, the majority of schools offer pupils a programme of social and personal education, and the work associated with this may well fall to teachers from a range of disciplines. Another area is remedial teaching of pupils with special needs (see later section in this book).

Schools are organised into forms or tutor groups and most teachers have a tutorial role in addition to their teaching commitment. There are opportunities for promotion to the responsibilities of head of year groups, head of lower or upper school, deputy or headteacher. These posts may entail responsibilities for:

- discipline in the school;
- curriculum planning;
- liaison with primary schools and local industry;
- timetabling and general administration.

Increments are paid to teachers for extra pastoral or management responsibilities. Teachers do get recognition of their contribution to a school over a period of time, even if they have had no increase in responsibility, because of the extended basic teaching pay scale.

There are limited opportunities as advisers and inspectors of schools, and as lecturers on teacher training courses. Other possibilities include becoming an education officer for a museum or field centre, or teaching abroad.

Teaching in further education

Teaching and lecturing in further education is varied work. Further education colleges include those which specialise in agriculture and horticulture, commerce or art and design, as well as colleges which provide a wide range of vocational and academic courses. A typical college might offer courses in catering, engineering, construction, business studies and general subjects (at GCSE, GNVQ and A level), taught by a wide range of full-time and part-time staff.

Because many of the courses are vocational, colleges are linked closely to local industry and many of the lecturers themselves have had industrial experience. Most courses offered in FE colleges are not high-level (beyond A level), but there are some Higher National Diploma and Certificate courses and, increasingly, colleges may offer the first year of a degree course in collaboration with a university or college of higher education. Some high-level qualifications are also offered on behalf of professional associations. Many colleges run 'access to higher education' (Access) courses for mature students.

The age range of students in FE varies from 16-year-olds to pensioners. These days, some courses run through what were traditionally college holiday times. Some evening work (including teaching) may be expected.

Besides actually teaching, lecturers have to do a lot of planning, preparation, assessing and marking. They will need to keep their industrial and commercial knowledge up to date, and maintain contacts with local employers. Senior lecturers and heads of department will be involved in administration and finance too.

Teaching academic subjects

Lecturers teaching on GCSE, GNVQ and higher-level courses will usually have a degree in their subject. It is not obligatory to take a Postgraduate Certificate in Education, but it may be advisable in terms of improving your teaching skills, and your chances of getting a job. Some postgraduate education courses with FE options are offered at universities and colleges of higher education. These courses are variations on the standard PGCE courses (i.e. those for school teaching). It is not guaranteed, however, that these courses can arrange teaching practice in FE colleges.

Those who take a postgraduate FE teacher training course do not automatically gain qualified teacher status (QTS), which is necessary to teach in schools and sixth-form colleges, but can do so by further training under the Licensed Teacher Scheme.

Scientific and technical graduates generally stand a better chance of finding a post than those with arts and social sciences degrees.

Teaching vocational courses

The range of qualifications judged suitable for those intending to teach students on vocational courses is very varied. Experience of industry or a relevant trade is essential in most departments. The exact qualifications required depend on the content and level of individual courses. In catering, for example, a lecturer might have an HCIMA (Hotel, Catering and Institutional Management Association) diploma, a home economics diploma or degree, or perhaps a degree in food science. On the practical side, he or she may hold City & Guilds qualifications or a high-level NVQ, together with a wide range of practical experience.

Many vocational courses are now competence-based. This means the lecturer has to assess the student's ability to carry out a particular practical task rather than just teach the theory.

Some colleges employ people as **instructors** on vocational courses, particularly the more practical subjects, on a lower pay scale than lecturers.

It is not necessary for lecturers in vocational subjects to have a pre-service teaching qualification, but there are full-time and in-service training courses for those with good technical or industrial qualifications and background, but no experience of teaching.

TRAINING COURSES

As well as the PGCE courses mentioned above, one-year full-time pre-service teacher training courses resulting in a Certificate in Education (Further Education) are offered at the Universities of Wolverhampton and Greenwich, and Bolton Institute of HE. These are open to graduates, or people with high-level vocational qualifications. Specialist subjects such as mathematics, science, business studies and engineering can be taken. These courses are outside the central applications scheme which covers other postgraduate teaching courses, and you would need to apply individually to the colleges concerned.

Part-time courses for unqualified teachers in FE, also leading to a Certificate in Education or the City & Guilds 730 award and other qualifications, are also available, but they do not attract mandatory awards. It is becoming increasingly important to acquire teaching qualifications, whether through the full-time or part-time route, to stand a good chance of promotion. In-service training is often funded by the employing college.

EMPLOYMENT OPPORTUNITIES

Employment prospects may be difficult in the next few years, particularly with FE colleges keeping tight reins on their budgets since becoming independent from LEA management. However, training credit schemes, Modern Apprenticeships and other developments may offer expanded opportunities in teaching vocational courses, general studies, numeracy, literacy, personal effectiveness, and other pre-vocational subjects.

Jobs in FE are advertised in the local press, the *Times Educational Supplement* and the education section of the *Guardian* (Tuesday edition). If you have a particular skill to offer to a vocational course, it would be advisable to contact the relevant head of department in any FE college in your area, with brief details of your qualifications and experience, as there may be part-time work available. This opportunity has dwindled somewhat, through tighter budgeting and the efforts of college managers to increase the teaching hours timetabled for full-time lecturers and instructors.

There are opportunities for part-time work in adult education in academic, vocational and recreational classes. Most colleges have an adult education organiser to whom enquiries could be directed.

Private sector further education
Many general and vocational colleges (e.g. 'crammers', language schools, secretarial colleges) operate outside the state sector. Requirements concerning staff vary enormously, and you would need to make individual enquiries.

TEACHING ART

A rt is a subject taught at all levels in schools and colleges. The term *art* includes such areas as fine art, graphic design, pottery, textiles, embroidery and photography. Primary teachers teach art alongside all other subjects in the curriculum, but art teachers in secondary and further education are specialists in their field.

Teaching in primary schools

In primary schools, art and design form an important part of the education of younger children. A member of staff with a particular interest may organise this side of the school's work, but normally all teachers will contribute. Often, creative work is done as part of a *project*, rather than just as a subject labelled 'art'. Much of the teacher's aim is to provide opportunities for children to experience different approaches to art, craft and design, using a variety of materials, in order to develop their creative and imaginative skills and their representation of ideas and feelings. The national curriculum for art also requires that children should be introduced to the works of artists, craftspeople and designers.

Teaching in secondary schools

Teaching art and design in secondary schools is a job for specialists. Art is taught as a discrete subject to all pupils up to the age of fourteen in all secondary schools in England and Wales. As a subject, it may be taught within a design or an expressive arts department. Pupils in secondary schools are introduced to a

wide range of art and design techniques and methods, which may include sculpture, work in wood and metal, textiles, pottery, printing techniques and photography. Many older pupils will be working for GCSE and A level examinations in art and design. The department may also teach history of art for examination courses.

Whilst ability in their specialist subject is naturally very important for intending teachers, being able to communicate ideas and enthusiasm to children is even more essential. Like all teachers, the teacher of art must be able to deal with unenthusi-astic and difficult pupils as well as the keen ones. Most teachers in secondary schools are expected not only to teach their own subject, but also to take part in the general life of the school, probably acting as a group tutor, and teaching other subjects if required. Experienced and well-qualified school teachers may go on to be heads of department or school inspectors.

Teaching in further and higher education

Lecturers must be competent and experienced artists or design-ers. In the vocational areas of design (fashion, industrial, graph-ics, etc) they will have had a good range of commercial experience. Many lecturers combine their own creative work with part-time teaching. Unlike teachers in schools, they do not need to have undertaken teacher training, although increasingly this is expected. There are also limited opportunities for people to teach on teacher training courses.

Opportunities exist for teaching art and craft subjects as leisure activities, either through evening classes, private day/weekend classes or 'activity' holidays. There seems to be more demand for teachers of *craft*work, such as batik, silkscreen printing, pot-tery, or stained glass work, rather than fine art.

GETTING STARTED IN ART TEACHING

Applications to some PGCE courses which specialise in art and design are dealt with through the Graduate Teacher Training Registry, while others (secondary only) are handled by the Art and Design Admissions Registry. It is sometimes possible to undertake a PGCE art and design course after a degree in a non-art subject, but only if you have considerable art and design experience.

Requirements for a degree in art and design subjects are either two or more A levels plus an art foundation course or an

Advanced GNVQ qualification in Art and Design (or the equivalent). See the book on *Art and Design* in the *Just the Job!* series for further details of art education.

Adults with few or no qualifications wanting to train for teaching could consider following an Access course. These courses are offered at many further education colleges and are specially designed as an alternative to GCSEs and A levels for entry to degree and other higher education courses (minimum age varies between 21 and 24 years). Admissions tutors may look for school subject relevance in any A level courses taken, or in the Access course content, for entry to primary level teacher training.

TEACHING BUSINESS STUDIES

Business studies as a school subject has become increasingly popular with young people, who may opt to study the subject from Intermediate GNVQ up to A level. It is seen by them as being very relevant to the adult world of work. For teachers, it can be quite a challenge, as a lot of the work is active and project-based, and neither pupils nor teacher know exactly where the project may lead them. Virtually all new entrants to teaching need a degree.

Teaching in schools

Most business studies teaching is restricted to pupils aged fourteen and over, and much of it is with post-16 students. Course content has moved away from covering the straightforward office skills and procedures, to more practical, entrepreneurial activities involving decision-making and problem-solving. Students look at every angle of business organisation; from locating the factory, employing the staff, finding out what customers want, producing and marketing the product(s), to the financial and legal aspects of operating a business. Teachers have to produce fairly imaginative teaching materials, often seeking assistance from local companies.

The business studies department is usually closely linked with design technology – often they operate as one department. There are obvious connections between designing and making a product, and running the business which markets, sells and services that product. There is also likely to be cooperation with

teachers of computing, economics and modern languages, as IT, statistical and foreign language skills have become of vital importance to businesses operating within the European Union frame. Exams and project work test students' ability with words, numbers and graphs – their ability to interpret raw facts and figures.

Teachers work with pupils who are taking GCSE, A or AS levels or Intermediate/Advanced GNVQs in business, as well as those who are not seeking qualifications in the subject, but for whom some aspects of business studies are a useful preparation for life after school.

Teaching in further education

In colleges of further education, the work of the teacher or lecturer is mainly directed towards preparing students for exams – again, GCSE, GNVQs, and A levels, and other vocational qualifications such as RSA, City & Guilds, Pitmans, etc. There is no compulsion for lecturers in further education to have teaching qualifications, but, increasingly, they are asked for. You will certainly need vocational qualifications in your subject, and firsthand experience of commerce or industry.

Teaching in higher education

At more advanced levels, there are opportunities for teaching business studies in universities and colleges of higher education. These are posts for academics who pursue their own research, as well as teaching students on degree courses.

TEACHING DESIGN & TECHNOLOGY

Design and technology, as a school subject, involves designing and making objects from all kinds of materials in the workshop. Virtually all new entrants to teaching are graduates. There are opportunities for adults with some higher education and industrial experience to undertake a shortened teacher training course.

Teaching in primary schools

In primary schools, design and technology form an important part of the education of younger children. A member of staff with particular interest or expertise in the subject may organise this side of the school's work, but normally all teachers will contribute. Often creative work takes the form of a project under the subject title *design and technology*. Much of the teacher's aim is to create opportunities for children to develop their design and technology capability through designing and making use of a wide variety of materials.

Teaching in secondary schools

Teaching design and technology in secondary schools is a job for specialists. The national curriculum lays down what pupils must study. Importance is placed on the teaching of design as a practical means of problem-solving. In schools, design and technology can be taught alongside art and craft subjects, within the scope of science, or as its own subject area. Within a design department, there are likely to be teachers of art, of design technology and, often, of home economics – perhaps including

specialists in metal, wood, plastics, textiles and fashion, food and graphics.

Pupils in secondary schools are introduced to a wide range of skills and techniques associated with designing and making, and requiring a knowledge of materials and processes. As well as practical and design work, the department may teach history of design, and theoretical principles of design for examination courses.

Together with ability in their specialist subject, teachers must be able to communicate ideas and enthusiasm to children, and deal with unenthusiastic and difficult pupils, as well as the keen ones. Experienced and well-qualified school teachers may go on to be heads of department, subject advisers, teacher training lecturers, or school inspectors.

Teaching in further and higher education

Lecturers must be competent and experienced technicians or designers, with relevant technical or academic qualifications and some knowledge of industry. They need not have undertaken teacher training, although, increasingly, this is expected. There are also limited opportunities for people to teach on teacher training courses.

Other opportunities exist for teaching craft subjects as leisure activities to adults (and sometimes to children), either through evening classes or private day or weekend courses.

TEACHING ENGLISH & DRAMA

There are jobs for teachers of English in all secondary schools and colleges, and many institutions also employ drama teachers. Some schools regard drama as a branch of English and prefer their staff to get involved in both areas. English is always one of the largest departments, as it is a core subject within the national curriculum, whilst drama is much smaller. New entrants to teaching are virtually all graduates.

Teaching in primary schools

Although primary schools don't have jobs for people who *only* teach English or drama, there are plenty of opportunities to work with children on language and communication skills. In primary schools, every teacher is an English teacher, and drama is an important way of helping children to learn and develop. Some specialisation is possible: you may see jobs advertised for teachers wanting to take special responsibility for *'language'* in primary and middle schools. This means being the school's 'expert' on that area of work, a resource upon which the other members of staff can draw, and you might be paid at a higher point on the salary scale. To be selected for that sort of post, you would need to be an experienced teacher and to have attended various in-service training courses, for example, on techniques of teaching reading.

Teaching in secondary schools

In secondary schools, teaching English and/or drama can cover a very wide range of activities. One lesson might be with a group of thirty eleven-year-olds, talking about writing stories; the next period, you might have a much smaller class doing A level English literature, or theatre studies. Then there is all the GCSE teaching for Years 10 and 11 – and 'retake' classes in the sixth form for people who are anxious to improve their GCSE grade. Some pupils will love your subject; some will hate it. But, whatever their feelings, it's the teacher's job to try to get the best from all pupils.

English is a very lively subject area. Although grammar and literature are still important components of English coursework, they are not the only topics! Because the subject concerns communication, English teachers can find themselves involved in all sorts of activities which you might not connect with English. For instance, English departments often help with work experience projects for older pupils – teaching pupils to write suitable letters to employers; developing their oral skills through discussion of their work experience; writing logbooks, diaries, summaries and so on. These days, a lot of use is made of information technology, too.

Drama plays an important role in helping pupils to develop self-confidence and imagination. It is not all that widely available as an examination subject in schools and so there is less requirement for drama teachers than for many other subject areas. However, it's often a very popular subject and at sixth form level there seems to be a growing interest in A level courses such as **theatre studies**.

Young people who are interested in popular/technical writing or news reporting through the media of journals, newspapers, videos or films may select **media studies** as an option. Note, however, that this subject is more consistently offered by further education colleges than by schools.

Teaching in further education

In colleges of further education, the work of the teacher or lecturer is mainly directed towards preparing students for exams – again, GCSE and A levels, and also subjects like English for business. Some students follow a course in English or communications as part of media studies or as an additional module to engineering.

At more advanced levels, there are opportunities for teaching in universities and colleges of higher education. These are posts for academics who pursue their own research, as well as teaching students on degree and postgraduate courses.

In the area of drama, besides the routes described earlier, there are various courses at specialist drama colleges; but you would still need to take a teacher training course if you wanted to teach in a state school.

TEACHING FOREIGN LANGUAGES

With increasing opportunities to train and work abroad, particularly within the European Union, modern foreign languages have a high priority in secondary schools. In order to continue to improve our ability to speak to the rest of the world, more teachers are needed, both to offer a full range of foreign language options and to increase pupil-teacher contact.

Fun to be fluent?

It can be exciting to send and receive secret messages, but frustrating if you can't crack the code. In a similar way, it can be fun and rewarding to learn another language, to make sense of what seemed to be gobbledygook and to be understood when using the language yourself. As international communication expands, it becomes more important to have a working knowledge of a language other than your own.

British people have a poor record in learning foreign languages – perhaps because we've got used to most other nationalities trying to speak English. Membership of the European Union has helped to change this attitude, forcing us to realise that foreign language skills are essential. Exchange visits to twinned schools, trips abroad in school parties, cheaper package holidays and satellite broadcasting have all increased young people's awareness of different cultures and the value of clear communication.

The need for communication

Communication is essential for British firms to be able to compete successfully with those of other countries. Employers are increasingly interested in a job applicant's language skills. Many firms which are expanding their business in Europe now expect their staff, at all levels, to take intensive training courses in an EU language, if they want promotion within the organisation.

All secondary schools must now offer at least one European Union language. Pupils can opt to study a foreign language to GCSE level, or as a short course. Today, modern language teachers are particularly sought after, and there is a trend to teach other languages besides French.

Although foreign languages are not required by the national curriculum for primary schools, some do offer some language teaching through projects on other countries, or club activities. Primary teachers with a modern languages degree might be an asset to a primary school.

What it takes to teach languages

In language teaching, there is now an emphasis on the culture and politics of the country. Much of the material used as a basis for oral work, listening exercises and reading is topical, and has to be continually revised and added to. In mixed ability groups, where there are always a few slower or more reluctant learners, a teacher has to be a skilled communicator and able to keep discipline. You need lots of physical and mental energy, patience and a keen sense of humour. You will also be expected to be fully involved in school exchanges and trips abroad.

Teaching pupils of all ages is helped by a little acting ability, and this can be used to good effect when encouraging students to attempt drama and role-play in a foreign language. Motivating mature students who have opted to learn a foreign language for holiday travel or for their work is seldom a problem.

Although traditional whole-class teaching methods are still used, language teaching often also takes place within small groups or with individual students using language laboratory facilities.

For a one-year PGCE course, you have to apply through the Graduate Teacher Training Registry. To train as a modern language teacher, it is important to have spent some time in the country of the particular language. A period of study abroad is usually included in modern language degree courses. Teachers are often expected to offer two languages, the second having been studied at least to A level. If you hold a joint honours degree in a modern language and another subject, you should make an early check that a particular teacher training establishment will accept the qualification as meeting their entry requirements.

You may be accepted for postgraduate teacher training without a degree, but with an equivalent-level qualification in your language. Check carefully with individual institutions.

Adults with graduate-level language qualifications and relevant work experience can apply for a place on a PGCE course, or become a licensed teacher, working in a school to achieve Qualified Teacher Status. Licensed teachers need to be over 24 (unless teacher-trained overseas) with at least two years' successful full-time higher education and GCSE grade C in English and mathematics, and able to demonstrate their suitability and aptitude.

Native speakers teaching modern languages

People from overseas who wish to teach their own language (or another foreign language) in Britain may do so if they meet certain criteria, including demonstrating competence in English and maths equivalent to GCSE grade C. European Union residents will normally find their teaching qualifications are accepted in this country, but will have to apply to the DFEE

(Department for Education and Employment) for QTS. People from outside the EU may have to check the acceptability of their degree with NARIC (the National Academic Recognition Centre) before applying for postgraduate training.

There are some PGCE courses in ethnic community languages.

TEACHING HUMANITIES

The humanity subjects taught in schools are usually history, geography and religious studies. These subjects cover the study of people, where and how they live and behave, their environment and beliefs, looking at past events as well as the present. History and geography are foundation subjects in the national curriculum, which means they are both compulsory for all pupils between the ages of 5 and 14 years old. Religious studies is also part of the basic curriculum and therefore compulsory for all pupils up to 18 years old, unless parents elect to withdraw their children from religious education classes.

Qualified Teacher Status in the humanities is achieved either through a BEd (Bachelor of Education degree) with history, geography or religious studies as a main subject, or a subject degree plus postgraduate teacher training.

Teaching history

History in schools covers a broad range of topics which can include political, economic, technical and scientific, social, cultural and religious matters in this country and abroad. It needs to be made interesting and relevant to pupils of all ages. Fieldwork, visits and using archive material can make history come alive for pupils.

There are a few posts for well-qualified historians to become lecturers and researchers in universities and other institutions of higher education. Teaching of students on degree and higher degree courses is carried out alongside research. Such historians publish their work, which is mainly used by the academic community.

Teaching geography

Geography gives a valuable understanding of how the world works. Pupils need to have a good grasp of physical, human and environmental geography as well as valuable day-to-day skills such as map-reading. Investigation and fieldwork form an important part of geography teaching. Geography teachers can go on to become managers of field study centres.

Teaching religious studies

Religious studies helps us to understand what different people believe and do – what is most important to them, what they value, what makes them tick. It helps us to assess what other people are saying, to describe an idea or a position different from your own, to work out another person's values and priorities. To teach this subject you need to be sympathetic to many other points of view; be able to explain things clearly; have imagination and a sense of humour.

Teachers in church schools are often expected to have an extra teaching qualification. The Catholic Teacher's Certificate and the Certificate in Religious Studies for Church of England Teachers of Religious Education are available at a number of colleges of higher education.

TEACHING MATHEMATICS & SCIENCE

The school-leaver who is most welcome in the employment market is the one with mathematics and science GCSEs at grade C or above. The problem lies in finding enough people to teach these subjects in schools. The government is actively seeking to encourage mathematics and physics graduates to enter teacher training.

Mathematics matters!

Mathematics and science are subjects which are vitally important to our future. Little progress can be made in industry, communications, agriculture, health, and care for the environment, without able scientists and technologists who have a good grasp of mathematics.

Teaching in schools

The vast majority of specialist maths and science teachers work in secondary schools and further education, but maths and science also play a very important part in the primary school, helping to lay firm foundations for later education.

Shortage of teachers

There is a shortage of maths and science teachers (especially physics), with industry being able to tempt maths and physics graduates away from teacher training courses by offering higher salaries. Secondary school rolls are stable, and rising in some areas, but there is a surge in primary schools numbers which will result in a need for more teachers by the end of the century.

Those who do train to teach maths and physics usually have a wide choice of vacancies and can often choose where they want to work. Promotion opportunities may also be more available to them in comparison with teachers of other subjects.

Biology teachers will find there is rather more competition for jobs and fewer promotion posts. If you are a biologist, it is certainly an advantage to offer a second science, as science is now usually taught as an integrated subject below A level.

Trends in teaching

Mathematics and science teaching in secondary schools today take an investigative, practical approach. In science, combined or integrated science courses are being offered to the age of 16, rather than separate physics, chemistry and biology, reflecting the way that sciences overlap in research and development. Some schools offer modular courses. Single science courses are remaining at A level and are available for some GCSE students. GNVQs in science and technology are also offered by schools and colleges.

Science teachers spend a lot of their time teaching in laboratories, and practical work is a major element of coursework. This means that planning and preparation must be thorough. Safe methods of working and observance of safety rules are very important, as dangerous chemicals, heat and electricity are regularly used.

For those not qualified to train as teachers, there are jobs as **laboratory assistant/technician** (see page 78).

Teaching in further education

Maths and science teachers also work in further education. They might teach on GCSE, GNVQ and A level courses, or provide 'service' courses in basic maths and science to vocational courses such as hairdressing, engineering, pre-nursing, construction, etc. Some higher-level courses are also taught in FE colleges, such as Higher National Diplomas or, increasingly, the first year of a degree course offered in conjunction with a higher education institution. There are openings for maths and science graduates (specialist PGCE courses are available) and for people with an industrial or applied science/engineering background.

TEACHING MUSIC

Teaching music encompasses a wide range of possible occupations. It can mean rehearsing the local choir one evening a week, on a voluntary basis, for a Christmas production of carols or Handel's Messiah; teaching a few viola pupils in your own home; working as a peripatetic instrumental teacher at several schools in the locality; working with people with special needs through the medium of music; taking large classes of pupils in theory of music; or lecturing undergraduates in a college of music – to give just a few examples. Formal music qualifications are not necessary to teach the subject in primary schools.

People who have trained as musicians work in primary, secondary and special schools; in colleges of music, colleges of further and higher education and universities; in music centres; and as private music teachers. Teachers of musical instruments can be appointed as **peripatetic** staff, visiting pupils in several schools.

Teaching music can be a huge commitment if you have a full-time position in a large secondary school where there is enthusiasm for your subject. You may well find yourself taking the whole school for hymn practice, giving singing lessons to large classes, taking groups for music theory, teaching keyboard playing to thirty pupils, having percussion sessions with the younger classes and taking small instrumental groups during the day. Out of school hours, there will also be the school orchestra to

conduct and manage, Christmas productions and Spring concerts to rehearse and, just possibly, a summer production of *Joseph and his Technicolour Dreamcoat*! You have to be enthusiastic about all aspects of music-making, at all levels of proficiency!

Music teachers in secondary schools must be trained and qualified to teach. This means either taking a Bachelor of Education degree for teaching music or taking a PGCE course, after a degree in music. BA or BMus degrees are academic degrees in which music history, methods of composition, musicology, knowledge of instruments and conducting techniques are studied. Performance and composition may form part of some degrees. Minimum entry requirements are two A levels plus five GCSEs at grade C (including mathematics and English). One of the A levels should normally be music. In addition, a high standard of musical ability is necessary; usually grade 8 on the main instrument and grade 5 or 6 on a second instrument.

Caroline – peripatetic music teacher

❛ I chose the path of peripatetic teaching in state schools, partly so that I could organise a part-time working week around my family commitments, and partly because I wanted to reach enthusiastic children whose families probably could not afford to pay the full price of private music lessons. My own children are still very small, and I am able to work half a full timetable of teaching sessions. This year, however, it has proved difficult to make up a half-time workload because schools have cut back the number of teaching sessions which they are willing to fund on behalf of their pupils. This problem exists all over the country, not just in this county, and has gradually become more acute since schools took over the running of their budgets, and made radical decisions about offering a full range of instrumental music lessons to their pupils – once provided through the county council.

I usually visit two schools each day, teaching groups of four or five young players of the same standard in each class. There are always problems to sort out at the beginning of a session – broken strings, bows needing repair, poor chin rests, besides the basic tuning and setting up of music stands which must be sorted out for each class.

Besides the groupwork on bowing technique, fingering, practising of scales and arpeggios, we work together on set pieces for the Royal College of Music grade examinations. We have breaks from playing when we repeat rhythms through clapping, sing different intervals and do aural exercises. Beginner players make great progress when they are learning familiar tunes and already can *hum them. Carols are a case in point! I have to complete reports on all my pupils each year, and have to be available at one location for consultations with individuals' parents.*

In my county, I also have responsibility for conducting a string orchestra of beginner players which meets once a week to rehearse a programme of two concerts each year. We have pieces especially commissioned for us from modern composers. These works often include a percussion group which helps the whole 60-strong orchestra keep together. Great fun, but trying on days when I feel tired by 4.00pm! When I hear the fully rehearsed sound the group achieves after several weeks of hard work, it all seems worthwhile! **'**

Anybody can set up as a private music teacher, but the most reputable have very good qualifications, and are listed in the Incorporated Society of Musicians' Register of Professional Private Music Teachers. Successful private teachers can earn a comfortable living, but many find that much of their work is done at weekends and in the evenings, i.e. outside normal school and working hours.

TEACHING SPORT & PE

Teachers of physical education work mostly in secondary schools, teaching games, gymnastics, dance, athletics, swimming and outdoor activities, such as canoeing and rock climbing – the range varies between individual schools. They also organise matches and help with extracurricular clubs.

Teaching in schools

Physical education in schools is concerned both with encouraging pupils' skills and body management and with young people's healthy growth and development. It is also a useful preparation for the management of leisure as adults.

Commonly, PE specialists teach another subject – this could be any one of the curriculum options, but it is useful to offer a mainstream subject. Of course, all primary school teachers have the scope to teach PE, games and movement to younger children, but this section focuses on teaching PE as a specialist subject.

PE teachers need to like and understand children and teenagers, and need to want to help them develop. A friendly but firm manner, patience, energy and organising skills are required. Fitness and skill in sport and movement are also very important. You are likely to spend a lot of time in out-of-school activities. After-school and Saturday matches, practices and clubs are all part of the job, besides the usual marking and lesson

preparation, duties of a form teacher, etc. You may be responsible for pupils studying PE up to GCSE and A level standard.

Both state and independent schools can place a very high emphasis on PE, sport and team games, and specialist posts are frequently advertised. Managing teams is an important part of the work, with a considerable commitment to midweek and weekend matches. Whilst there is no legal requirement for teachers in independent schools to have had formal teacher training (as there is in state schools), many independent schools insist on teachers being qualified and capable of teaching an additional subject.

Specialist training for graduates wishing to teach PE is available in a number of universities and colleges. Some of these courses may be taken after any degree, although some institutions prefer students who have taken PE, sports science or human movement as at least a major part of their undergraduate course. There is also evidence that employment prospects are better for students who have taken one of these subjects as their first degree. A limited number of one-year postgraduate courses are provided through school-centred initial teacher training courses.

Some PE and dance applicants may be accepted on to a BEd course with one A level, if they offer an extremely high standard in their practical subject.

For PE teaching, clearly a high level of physical fitness is demanded, and adult applicants need to be aware that their career opportunities could be very limited.

PROSPECTS

On the whole, people with a relevant degree plus a PGCE qualification from a university seem to have least difficulty in finding employment. Being able to offer a second teaching subject that is in demand will improve chances of getting a job. You should also think ahead to when you are older – as the physical aspects of the job become less attractive and more arduous, an alternative teaching subject will almost certainly be required (one of the current 'shortage' subjects, of sciences, mathematics, modern languages and design technology, would be ideal).

Other openings

Sports coaching at sport and leisure centres does not demand such high academic qualifications, but you will be expected to have appropriate practical qualifications in your chosen sport or sports.

TEACHING PEOPLE WITH SPECIAL NEEDS

Specialist teachers work with pupils with special needs – that is children with physical disabilities, moderate or severe learning difficulties, visual impairment, behavioural problems, etc. They may work in special schools or in special units within ordinary schools. Most special schools are run by local education authorities, but some are controlled by voluntary groups such as the Shaftesbury Society and the Rudolf Steiner organisation. Virtually all new entrants to teaching are graduates, and most specialist teachers have a few years' teaching experience before they move into this area of education.

Teaching in schools

Children with special educational needs are increasingly educated in ordinary schools, and *every* school must now appoint its own **special needs coordinator** (SENCO). The SENCO is normally a teacher who accepts additional responsibility to take on this role, except in very large secondary schools where an extra member of staff may be appointed. Teachers attend in-service training courses to improve their skills and knowledge in the field of special education. Sometimes schools have special units, to cater for children with moderate learning difficulties, for example, who need a special curriculum and learning environment.

However, children with certain types of disability, such as deafness, blindness or very severe intellectual or physical disabilities, are most likely to receive appropriate education and care in special schools and colleges. Provision in special schools or units is also made for children with emotional or behavioural difficulties.

Some teachers employed by local authorities are 'peripatetic'. That means they travel from one school to another to give special help – for example, to one or two deaf children in each ordinary school in their area.

What it takes

Teachers in special education require all the personal qualities needed by any successful teacher, only even more so! Patience and perseverance are very important – it often takes children with disabilities a very long time to master a skill. This means covering the same ground over and over again, but in different ways. Resourcefulness and imagination are essential. Sympathy for pupils' difficulties must go hand in hand with firmness and a constructive approach, so that you can give them the best chance of overcoming their problems. This also applies to teaching children with social/behavioural problems.

TRAINING TO TEACH IN SPECIAL EDUCATION

To work in any state school you need Qualified Teacher Status (QTS) – either through a BEd (Bachelor of Education degree), or through any other degree relevant to the national curriculum, plus a PGCE (Postgraduate Certificate in Education). All initial teacher training courses include a limited amount of special needs work.

Teachers of any pupils with special needs should first have experience of working in mainstream schools with mainstream pupils, so special education is not a 'first' career entered straight from college, but a specialism one moves into after a few years.

It is compulsory to obtain a specialist qualification to teach blind or deaf/partially hearing children, and various full-time and part-time courses are available. Usually these are taken on an in-service or secondment basis by teachers with some experience.

For work with children or young people with other types of special needs, various in-service courses are available. Whilst these are not compulsory, they are likely to be a help in getting posts and seeking promotion. Once in a teaching post, your local education authority will be able to advise you on the availability of further training.

In addition, some of the voluntary organisations running special schools and colleges offer their own training schemes, which may follow a particular approach. Contact the specific organisations. Steiner schools employ both state-qualified and Steiner teachers.

Teaching older teenagers and adults

Various colleges of further education (both mainstream and special), and other centres, offer general education and/or vocational training to people with disabilities. They have a need both for general teachers and for those who can provide training in specific vocational skills (e.g. computing, engineering, handcrafts). As with schoolteachers, some staff will have specialist qualifications, and others will not. Training courses are available – both pre-entry and in-service.

The voluntary sector also runs homes, centres and communities for adults with special needs. In some, such as the Camphill communities, 'staff' live and work in the community alongside the residents.

Opportunities other than teaching

Teachers are not the only people who 'teach' children and adults with special needs. **Education support assistants** (see page 76) also work in schools. You could also consider work as a care assistant or nurse. These people can be very involved in teaching daily living skills to youngsters with physical or learning difficulties, for instance. Therapists also do work similar in some ways to teachers.

TEACHING OVERSEAS

There are various openings for people who wish to work as teachers overseas, including through voluntary service and teaching English as a foreign language (see next section). Opportunities exist for qualified and experienced teachers, and also for those without formal teaching qualifications.

Teaching in developing countries

This has declined as an area of work, with more developing countries now meeting their need for teachers from amongst their own graduates. One way is through Voluntary Service Overseas (VSO) – particularly for graduates or people with craft or technical qualifications. There are openings for people with and without teacher training, though a teaching qualification will offer more choice of country. Volunteers normally work for at least two years at local rates of pay, and should be aged between 20 and 70 (!) with no dependants. Maths, science, English language, and vocational skills such as secretarial, home economics and technical subjects, are most in demand. Jobs are mainly in secondary and technical schools, but there are also some primary, special education and teacher training posts. Volunteers receive intensive training.

Aid agencies and missionary societies recruit volunteers, though on a smaller scale. World Service Enquiry at Christians Abroad can give information – you don't have to be a Christian to use the service (see Further Information section).

Other posts for graduates and trained teachers are advertised in the educational press. Embassies may be able to help. The same range of subjects tends to be required, and posts are generally offered on limited contracts of up to three years. It may be possible to stay on longer, but there are very limited openings for permanent work.

Teaching English

This is one of the main areas of overseas work for teachers. Fortunately, English is a language that people are keen to learn. This area can be divided into three: teaching English as a foreign language (TEFL), teaching English for special purposes, such as business or industry (TESP); and teaching English as a second language (TESL) – see the next section for fuller details.

TEFL and **TESP** usually involve working for commercial language schools, and teaching adults or teenagers. Jobs can be permanent (though this is quite rare), on short-term contract, or seasonal. For example, the British Council employs people on fixed-term contracts of one to two years. It's possible to find TEFL work even if you are unqualified or inexperienced, but training is recommended. **TESL** is more often school-based, and is particularly important in countries where English is used in administration and communication between different language groups. This is an area where there is more chance of making a permanent career.

Permanent work abroad

Prospects for teachers wishing to emigrate or otherwise work abroad on a permanent basis are limited. Either because of an oversupply of native teachers, or because of nationality and national qualification requirements, there are difficulties for Britons wishing to work in the USA, Australia, Canada, New Zealand and European countries outside the EU.

Within the European Union, there are restrictions for UK-qualified teachers wishing to teach in some of the member states. For example, in several countries, teachers are classed as civil servants and must be nationals of that country. Some require a supplementary qualification. And, of course, most countries demand excellent language skills.

Teaching in international schools, independent schools overseas and European schools

There are some schools overseas which offer an international curriculum, and/or which teach through the medium of the English language. These include European Schools set up for the children of EU officials, schools belonging to the European Council of International Schools (actually not confined to Europe) and various independent schools. These schools typically offer posts to qualified and experienced teachers on a fixed-term contract basis, though there could be opportunities for permanent posts, especially in independent schools. Posts are found through agencies such as Gabbitas Educational Consultants Ltd (see Further Information section), through job adverts, or by writing to schools on lists available from embassies or high commissions.

English language assistants

English language assistants help with English conversation lessons in schools abroad. You need to be over 18, and it is preferable to have an A level in the language of the country you are going to (if European). Openings are available for modern language students, but also graduates in other subjects (especially linguistics or English).

This option is taken up by young people before their higher education, for their year abroad as part of a language degree, or after graduating. Opportunities are not confined to Europe – there are also openings in the Far East, South America and Russia. The Central Bureau for Educational Visits and Exchanges is the best contact.

Exchanges

Experienced teachers can consider an exchange for a term or a year with an overseas teacher. Opportunities are mainly in the European Union, Russia, North America and Commonwealth countries. The Central Bureau for Educational Visits and Exchanges can provide information (see Further Information section).

Other opportunities

Families requiring tutors also advertise, often in the *Times Educational Supplement* or the *Guardian*.

TEACHING ENGLISH AS A FOREIGN LANGUAGE

English is the number-one language of business and communications in the world, and is used as an official or semi-official language in more than seventy countries. Therefore, the demand to learn English worldwide is great. Teaching English as a foreign language (TEFL) is an opportunity that many people take to combine work with travel – teaching English to foreign students in schools and colleges in the UK and overseas.

TEFL – teaching English as a foreign language – occurs in both private and state sector colleges and schools which deal with large proportions of overseas students. Many organisations offering short holiday courses for adults and children employ TEFL teachers (not always qualified ones), though such posts are normally seasonal only. Some colleges of further education run courses in English for foreign students. However, *permanent* TEFL jobs are mainly in the most reputable private schools and colleges.

A lot of TEFL-trained teachers work abroad, though sometimes only on a temporary or seasonal basis. There are some very well-paid posts with companies overseas, as well as jobs in language schools, etc. There are also opportunities with voluntary agencies such as VSO, or religious organisations or with the British Council (see previous section on teaching overseas.)

TESP means **teaching English for special purposes** – technical terms to use within the fields of business, medicine or engineering, for example. TESP posts are based in language schools or specialist colleges. Short courses are offered to specific professions, and there may also be some in-company training offered. There is often a mixture of short and long courses available.

TESL means **teaching English as a second language**, usually to immigrants and others who wish to settle in an English-speaking country. The state sector is the normal employment field, with courses being run in colleges and institutions of further and higher education (both daytime and evenings), immigrant reception centres and, in certain areas with a high non-native population, within state schools. Much teaching is also done on a one-to-one basis in people's own homes, but this is mostly on an unpaid, voluntary basis by unqualified 'teachers'. Such experience could, however, be very useful to someone wishing to make a career in TESL.

TRAINING

For all kinds of English language teaching, teachers should have clear speaking voices, an extrovert personality and the ability to communicate successfully with people of all ages and from varying cultural backgrounds. English as a foreign language is usually taught in a lively way, attempting to simulate realistic situations of everyday life. Role-play and acting are used as techniques, and an interest in drama or entertainment is useful.

TEFL and TESP
All recognised private language schools require their staff to be graduates or the equivalent, and to be trained or undergoing training in TEFL. TEFL qualifications are equally suitable for TESP.

There are various ways of acquiring a TEFL qualification:

- Various postgraduate and/or post-experience courses are offered by universities and other institutions of higher education, ranging from one-term intensive courses to longer periods of study leading to higher degrees, etc (with several variants in between). These courses provide specialist study in, or relevant to, TEFL, but *do not result in fully qualified teacher status*. (Many people taking these courses would, however, already have taken an initial teaching course.)
- Short courses leading to the Royal Society of Arts/University of Cambridge Local Examinations Syndicate examinations (the most common in this field) and the Trinity College Licentiate (see below for explanation of these qualifications) are also offered in a number of state colleges: see the CRAC *Directory of Further Education* for their location. Unfortunately, students wishing to take these courses on a full-time basis are likely to have to find their own means of support and finance, since they fall into the discretionary category of awards as far as local education authorities are concerned.
- Some courses, usually leading to the RSA/UCLES qualifications mentioned above, are available on an evenings-only basis at colleges.
- It's possible to gain the RSA/Cambridge Diploma through distance learning.
- A number of the private colleges, which teach English as a foreign language, offer training courses. There are preparatory courses for beginners, usually lasting three or four weeks; and longer courses leading to the Royal Society of Arts Certificate. The longer courses are either about 10-12 weeks' intensive full-time study, or part-time courses, often for employees of the college who are already undertaking TEFL work, lasting one year at about two evenings' study per week. Students can expect to have to finance themselves.

- A number of language colleges offer their own 'in-house' training schemes which are not externally validated – i.e. there is no national examination at the end of the course. Nevertheless, some of these training schemes are highly acceptable within the English-language teaching world. Some courses of training may only be open to employees of that particular college, while others may be offered to anyone interested. In the latter case, the college may often recruit future teaching staff from amongst the best students. Assistance from public funds towards the cost of such courses is unlikely to be awarded.

TESL

Training in the teaching of English as a second language is basically confined to the state sector. However, some people initially trained in TEFL might move across to TESL work. TESL courses are available on the same basis as described in the first three points above.

QUALIFICATIONS IN TEFL/TESL

Royal Society of Arts (RSA)/University of Cambridge Local Examinations Syndicate (UCLES)

RSA/UCLES examinations are offered at two levels, and are the most widely recognised and available qualifications. The RSA/UCLES Certificate in Teaching English as a Foreign Language to Adults (CTEFLA) is the basic qualification, taken after a fairly short period of preparation (four weeks' full-time, five weeks' part-time). The RSA/UCLES Diploma, however, is a very tough examination – both theoretical and practical. It requires a great deal of preparation, and both practical and academic ability. It is a very widely acceptable qualification.

Trinity College, London

Trinity College offers the Certificate in the Teaching of English to speakers of other languages (TESOL), equivalent to the RSA/UCLES Certificate. It also offers a Licentiate Diploma in the Teaching of English as a Foreign or Second Language (TEFSL). It is not as widely available as RSA, though candidates can enter themselves privately for the examination. An Associate Diploma is also available for non-native speakers of English. There are some new qualifications in the pipeline, but not yet available in colleges.

English Speaking Board
The English Speaking Board has a qualification relevant to both TEFL and TESL, in the teaching of English as an acquired language. One can enter privately for this examination. A limited number of FE colleges offer this qualification.

Other diplomas, degrees, etc, awarded by universities and other colleges
The diplomas, certificates, Master of Arts degrees and so on, which can be taken in some universities and other institutions of higher education, vary so much that the syllabus of each should be examined carefully to see whether the content is really relevant to your particular requirements. The courses range from straightforward diplomas in TEFL/TESL, to courses in applied linguistics, phonetics, etc. The Postgraduate Certificate in Education courses, which include TEFL/TESL, can confer fully qualified teacher status.

NON-TEACHING JOBS IN SCHOOLS

Most schools, whether in the private or state sector, have some non-teaching staff. The number of posts will vary a lot from school to school. For instance, a large comprehensive school has administrative, welfare and laboratory staff, while an infant school secretary will be a 'jack of all trades', typing letters and doing minor first aid.

Schools are now responsible for their own budgets and administration, and have to provide lots of statistics for the annual 'league tables' and other purposes. There is also paperwork associated with the national curriculum. Many schools choose to employ more non-teaching staff in order to free teachers from some of this extra administrative and technical work.

Because many of the non-teaching jobs in schools are only part-time and have school holidays, they are often attractive to working parents. School secretary jobs, for example, may be quite difficult to obtain because of their popularity. Schools are normally responsible for recruiting their own staff and usually advertise in the local press if they have a vacancy. There are also a lot of non-educational staff employed in further education colleges. These jobs are more likely to be full-time, with periods of leave similar to local government holidays. Generally, there is much more administrative and technical support work to do in colleges than in schools.

School secretary

This is likely to be a full-time job in a larger school, but is often part-time in a small one. The work tends to follow school hours, but not necessarily full school holidays, and the job often goes to a mature person with good secretarial skills. There is clerical work in connection with school records, examination entries and filing, as well as typing and reception work.

Usually the school secretary's office is where visitors call first and where any queries are directed. The secretary in a small school often becomes a friend to the children and deals with grazed knees, nosebleeds and other minor ills and troubles. It may also be necessary to deal with angry or upset parents, so tact and diplomacy are valuable skills to have.

In a large school or college, there will be a number of secretaries. Some will be personal secretaries to people such as the college principal. Others will do more general work, similar to that described above.

Clerical assistant

In large schools and in colleges of further education, there is often sufficient work for full-time or part-time clerical assistants as well as secretaries. Such jobs may be suitable for young people. A school-leaver would usually be required to have a couple of GCSEs at grade C, including English, while an older person with some experience may not need any academic qualifications. (See also the book on *Office & Administrative Work* in the *Just the Job!* series.)

Administrative assistant or bursar

In a large school or college, there can be sufficient administrative work to justify employing a bursar. This is often true now that schools are responsible for their own financial affairs. The bursar's job is to organise the running of all the school's administration, particularly financial, but including a wide range of other duties. These might include administering the booking of school premises for extra-curricular activities or community use; checking on the state of the buildings and authorising minor repairs; dealing with the administration of staff pay and recruitment; preparing entry forms for external examinations; and organising school transport.

The job of bursar in an independent school is often taken by someone with an accountancy or banking type of background, and would include working out what the fees should be to ensure the school's survival.

Librarian and library assistant

It is not always necessary to be a qualified librarian to work as a school librarian. In some schools, librarians have the same status as a library assistant in a public library. They would be expected to have five GCSEs at grade C or equivalent, including English, and, even if the librarian did have professional qualifications, the pay would only be that of an assistant. But some schools do employ professional (graduate) librarians. Colleges of further education also generally employ professionally qualified librarians – a large college might have several. In very small schools, looking after the library might be part of the duties of a clerical assistant or one of the teachers.

Besides looking after books and other learning materials, librarians have a lot of contact with pupils and students, often teaching them to use the library's facilities. They may also be responsible for buying books and other resources. (See the book on *Information & the Written Word* in the *Just the Job!* series.)

Teaching assistant/classroom assistant/ education support assistant

Support assistants work in primary, secondary and special schools doing various jobs in order to give teachers more time to actually teach. Jobs for general support assistants might include preparing displays and setting out apparatus, helping children change for games or PE, and supervising in the playground, dining hall and cloakrooms.

Education support assistants' work is particularly important in special schools for children with physical and mental disabilities, where caring for the children is very demanding. There are also, increasingly, jobs for support assistants in mainstream schools to help children with special needs to integrate and cope with the demands of an ordinary school day. This is a growing area, as more children with disabilities are educated in ordinary schools. In this case, the support assistant usually works with one child with special needs, rather than being a general help to the teacher. Such jobs are often part-time.

Several colleges are now running one-year part-time courses for **specialist teaching assistants** (STAs). STAs help teachers in primary schools with reading, writing and maths. Course applicants should have GCSE grade C in English and maths (or equivalent), or they may be accepted after interview or a test.

Escort on school transport

Escorts are employed to look after some children travelling daily to and from special schools. These children usually have fairly severe physical or mental disabilities. The escorts are responsible for the children from the time they leave their home until they are handed over to the school and from school to home. They have to be very careful to know of alternative places to take the child if, for any reason, the parent is not there to look after them. This is a part-time job only.

Matron and assistant matron

These are usually boarding school jobs. Matrons act as housekeepers and substitute parents to children away at boarding school. They are responsible for such things as bedding, laundry, hygiene, and the health of the children. The matron will usually have one or more assistant matrons and supervise the work of domestic cleaning staff. A matron could have a background in nursing or as a nursery nurse, or just the experience of having brought up a family. The main requirements are good organising ability, a friendly, approachable personality and patience. Assistant matrons are often drawn from students who have taken some kind of residential care course at a further education college.

Midday supervisory assistant

Midday supervisory assistants look after pupils during the lunch break at school. They supervise the dining room and, with young children, may cut up food or persuade the more awkward characters to eat their meal. They do not serve meals, lay tables or wash up. They supervise the pupils in the playground or inside during wet weather. Hours are normally very limited.

School meals service

The kitchen staff are generally part-timers and work on preparing, serving and washing up after school lunches. Many school kitchens now just heat and serve meals that have been cooked and chilled elsewhere. These jobs usually appeal to people with young families, for whom the hours of work are ideal. Supervisors are likely to have experience of mass catering, and may need to be able to make a little money go a long way. There is a great deal of difference between the supervisor's job in a small primary school and in an enormous comprehensive school. The supervisor in a large school will not only need to be an experienced caterer, but also to be capable of organising quite a large staff.

School crossing patrol

School crossing patrols supervise children crossing dangerous roads on their way to and from school. It is very much a part-time job, perhaps only an hour a day, but reliability on even the coldest and wettest mornings is essential!

Laboratory assistant/technician

Laboratory assistants look after the equipment and materials for the science departments of secondary schools. They set up experiments for teachers and clear up after practical sessions. They have to make sure that stocks of chemicals are kept up, that equipment is in working order and there is enough of it. They have to work very closely with the science teaching staff of the school. Some qualifications, especially in science subjects, would be required, at least to GCSE at grade C and commonly to A level or equivalent.

Information technology coordinator/ computer technician

IT technicians provide computer expertise for both teachers and pupils in larger secondary schools. They have the responsibility for making sure systems are 'up and running' throughout the school and for carrying out any necessary repairs and adjustments to equipment.

Audio-visual technician/resources technician

Audio-visual technicians look after all the technical sound, vision and printing or reprographic equipment in a school. The equipment used varies tremendously from school to school and could include items like closed circuit television, back projectors, cassette recorders, photocopiers, film projectors, videoplayers and recorders and complicated printing equipment.

Audio-visual technicians come from varied backgrounds and in fact the colleges which run courses for AV technicians say it is often very difficult devising courses for a group with such mixed abilities. If you had some experience in areas of work like photography, electronics, TV and radio repair or printing, you might well have a suitable background for a job as an AV technician. Most courses are part-time for those already working, but there are a few two-year full-time courses which lead to a BTEC National Diploma in Audio-Visual Design, which could be a useful qualification for this and other types of work in the communications and media industry.

Grounds staff

Grounds staff are usually responsible for sports pitches and school gardens, and possibly for greenhouses and cold frames used by rural studies departments. There will probably be only one member of grounds staff in each school and therefore an experienced person is required. Amenity horticulture or groundsmanship skills, perhaps with appropriate qualifications, would be useful.

Caretaker

School caretakers look after school buildings, oversee the work of the cleaners, and take responsibility for the security of the building and such things as the heating and plumbing. Often a house on the school site goes with the job, as caretakers may have to be available in the evenings for school events and let-tings, when they go round putting out lights, shutting windows and locking doors. This is a job for a mature person. It's not the sort of job for which you need any qualifications, but caretakers need to be practical and have plenty of common sense.

Cleaner

Most cleaners work less than twenty hours a week, and the average is about twelve hours a week. When a school needs a cleaner they will sometimes advertise locally, but more com-monly this work is contracted out. Cleaners usually work under the supervision of their firm's manager.

VACANCIES

Posts are usually advertised in the local press, but it is sometimes worth approaching heads of schools, particularly for jobs like midday supervisor and education support assistant, where smaller schools may not bother to advertise but rely on personal contact.

For school and college addresses, look in the telephone direc-tory under the local education authority – or under the names of individual independent or grant-maintained schools. Bursars, matrons and assistant matrons, and other jobs in independent schools are usually advertised in the national press, or you could contact the recruitment section of Gabbitas Educational Consultants Ltd, who carry a vacancies list for matron and other domestic posts.

OPPORTUNITIES OUTSIDE TEACHING FOR TRAINED TEACHERS

Teachers who want a change from teaching may wonder what scope there is for using their qualification. Some may want to use their teaching experience directly; others may wish to use the skills they have gained in a different field. This section is only intended as an ideas-generator.

The range of jobs divides basically into two categories:

- Posts in the educational world which are outside normal teaching and classroom work, but which build directly upon teaching experience. Many of these are 'promotion' posts.
- Jobs where you could use some of the skills developed in your teacher training or experience.

Posts in education
Teacher trainers, educational advisers and inspectors

Teacher trainers may work with students on initial teaching courses (BEds and PGCEs) as well as in-service courses for teachers with experience. In some colleges, you may be expected to teach students on courses other than education. You may lecture in your own subject, in educational method, or both. Often, experience of teaching a wide age range of children is desirable. More and more in-service training is now provided by self-employed **education consultants**.

Advisers in local education authorities (LEAs) usually have a specialist subject or age-range responsibility, as well as a general or geographical responsibility on behalf of the LEA. Their job is to ensure good standards are maintained. They are often involved with in-service training, keeping local teachers up to date with trends and practice in their subject area, and they also evaluate and monitor teaching methods.

A teacher may also become a registered **inspector**, and, as part of an independent team, work for OFSTED (the Office for Standards in Education) and the Department for Education and Employment to oversee the performance of schools and teachers, making reports and recommendations following their visits to establishments. If you work for the inspectorate, you must be prepared to be mobile and to accept postings more or less anywhere.

Special projects

Advertisements sometimes appear in the educational press for teachers to join special research projects. Usually short-term (say two or three years) and often not particularly well paid, these are likely to appeal to the ambitious teacher with a few years' experience and a lot of ideas and enthusiasm. This sort of job could just be a break in a teaching career or a stepping stone to advisory or training posts.

Education officer posts

These occasionally arise with museums, charities such as the RSPCA, and with nature conservation bodies – those whose activities already interest children and young people or which would like to attract young people. The job of an education officer may involve work with visiting parties of children, preparing materials for them (worksheets, exhibitions, nature trails, etc) and, perhaps, fund-raising and general publicity such as writing newsletters. Some professional bodies and organisations also have careers information and general schools liaison posts.

Educational administration

There may be opportunities with local authorities to administer some areas of educational finance (salaries, grants and allowances), and work on statistics and planning to ensure that the LEA's resources are used to best advantage. Administrators may budget for repairs to buildings and replacements or extensions, making sure the LEA complies with new legislation (e.g. the national curriculum), sorting out day-to-day problems referred by schools to the LEA. Administrative posts also occur in schools, colleges and universities, and with examination boards.

Additional specialisms

One possibility for a change of work is to acquire an additional specialism not generally offered in initial teacher training – for instance, careers guidance and education, counselling, computer studies or health education – and train through part-time study, distance learning or an in-service course to obtain a qualification.

Teaching in other situations

For teachers seeking a change but wanting to remain in teaching, it may be possible to change the subject you teach, or the age range, although a major move from infant to secondary would be difficult. This could involve retraining and opportunities may be limited. Teaching abroad, or teaching English as a foreign language, are other possibilities.

Another area into which **teachers** can move is education in a different setting. This includes special education (provision for children with impaired sight or hearing, learning difficulties or physical disability); centres for young offenders or young people with behavioural problems; prisons; the Armed Forces; industrial training. Often, experience of teaching in a 'normal' environment is thought to be desirable as a background to specialising in one of these areas.

Other posts which may make use of teachers' skills

Occupations using communication and persuasion skills

All successful teachers must be good communicators. Jobs include selling (retail management, insurance sales, publishers' representative), advertising and public relations, journalism, broadcasting, entertaining and training.

Caring work and work with children or young people
This covers a huge range of jobs, some more closely connected with education than others. Possibilities include: social work, youth work, educational and child psychology, church work, educational welfare work, creative therapies (music, dance, drama, art, etc), health and medical work (including nursing, paramedical careers like speech therapy and physiotherapy), careers advisory work, counselling (general, marriage guidance, young people's services, etc); work in the leisure industry, for example supervising young people on activity holidays, etc.

Making use of information-handling skills and academic abilities
Much will depend on your own academic background – different degree specialisms will suggest different possibilities. Some of the possibilities are librarianship, information officer or information management work, archives, technical writing, local government or civil service posts, broadcasting research, actuarial or statistical work.

WORKING IN TRAINING

There are two main types of work in training. Training officers, managers and consultants advise firms on the training needs of their staff and arrange for the training to be done. Trainers and instructors actually carry out the training themselves. A degree or equivalent may be necessary for higher-level jobs; otherwise vocational qualifications and the right skills and experience are likely to be as important as academic success.

Traditionally, most training work has happened in industry and commerce, carried out by technical training officers and instructors. In the last ten or fifteen years, government policy has resulted in more private training companies and organisations who sell training to employers. On the other hand, National Vocational Qualifications (NVQs) are often gained through training in the workplace. People are likely to have to retrain and learn new skills several times throughout their working lives in future, so prospects for trainers should be good.

Depending on what the job involves, training work can make use of a wide range of skills, including:

- **communication** – relating to, and motivating people;
- **teaching** – for those involved in direct training;
- **analysis** – diagnosing problems, suggesting solutions and setting objectives;
- **organisation** – planning and using time effectively.

Working as a training officer in industry and commerce

People are employed as training officers in many organisations, including banks, retailing companies, local and central government, industrial firms and training associations. Job titles vary; you may come across any of these:

Assistant training officer, training officer, training adviser, training manager, training and development manager, education officer, training professional, education and training officer, training coordinator, personnel and training manager, human resource/training consultant, staff development and training officer.

These titles do not necessarily describe a difference in job content, but jobs do vary considerably.

What the work involves

Training officers may:

- research the training needs of the staff in their organisation;
- develop training policy;
- ensure that training programmes are carried out;
- assess how effective training has been;
- develop training manuals and handbooks;
- train trainers and supervisors;
- instruct trainees themselves;
- provide advice on professional qualifications and career development;
- liaise with government and funding agencies.

Some posts may combine training officer work with other functions such as personnel work, recruitment and general management. Training posts are usually based within the personnel department.

Independent training work

Increasingly, independent training companies and individuals do a lot of work on a consultancy basis, or under contract, for a wide variety of firms and organisations. Many are currently under contract to provide training for government schemes. Commercial firms may use independent trainers to provide courses on specialised topics for employees. Naturally, trainers in this field will have good qualifications and wide experience in the areas of training that they are offering. There are opportunities for developing small businesses offering consultancy and contract training services.

Instructors and trainers

While much training in industrial and commercial organisations is done on-the-job by supervisory-level staff, many people are employed on a full-time basis as instructors and trainers. Instructors have a responsibility for teaching specific skills and expertise, both to new recruits and to people already in their posts. Jobs might be in the training departments of individual organisations, or at training centres or residential staff colleges.

The range of work done by instructors and trainers is very broad, and the backgrounds from which instructional staff come are varied. For instance, instructors who train engineering apprentices need to be skilled and experienced craftsmen/women or technicians. Those training bank staff, retail managers and shop staff, police officers, computer programmers and operators, would need to be professionals in their own sphere. Some trainers may train a wider range of personnel from various occupations, in areas such as communications, general management, marketing, selling and public relations.

Many instructor/trainer posts have very similar counterparts in colleges of further and higher education and private vocational training colleges.

GETTING STARTED IN TRAINING

Training work is rarely a first job for either school-leavers or college-leavers, or even for graduates. You must first gain some appropriate experience. However, if a young person is interested in the work, you should start with a degree (in any subject, though degrees in subjects such as psychology and education are useful), followed by posts in personnel work, teaching (especially further and adult education), general management, etc.

There are several ways of making a start in the field of training:

- by starting as an assistant in a personnel department, as personnel/human resource management is often closely linked to training (however, this is difficult to do without personnel qualifications);
- by starting as a training assistant in industry or commerce;
- by getting a training coordinator post within government-funded schemes for unemployed people (young people or adults);
- by first working as an instructor in an area of skill which you possess – for instance, in business or technology – and branching out into the wider area of training later;
- by working as a further education lecturer (perhaps part-time) in an area in which you are qualified. This will build up credibility and contacts with local employers, and you may also get the chance of gaining some training consultancy as a member of a college-based team.

PROFESSIONAL QUALIFICATIONS

The Institute of Personnel and Development (IPD) offers a range of qualifications for people already working in this field, including the Certificate in Training Practice. There are training and development NVQs at levels 3 and 4, and level 5 management NVQs have recently arrived. Other qualifications include postgraduate courses in training or human resource development. The IPD can advise on courses, or you can find information in handbooks of postgraduate qualifications, which may be available in college or public libraries. There are also City & Guilds and RSA qualifications in training and teaching vocational subjects.

FOR FURTHER INFORMATION

GENERAL

Art and Design Admissions Registry (ADAR) – Penn House, 9–10 Broad Street, Hereford HR4 9AP. Tel: 01432 266653.

CILT (Centre for Information on Language Teaching and Research) – 20 Bedfordbury, London WC2N 4LB. Tel: 0171 379 5101.

Design and Technology Association – 16 Wellesbourne House, Walton Road, Wellesbourne, Warwickshire CV35 9BR. Tel: 01789 470007. Produce a journal of *Design and Technology Education*.

The Geographical Association – 343 Fulwood Road, Sheffield S10 3BP. Tel: 0114 2670666.

Graduate Teacher Training Registry – Fulton House, Jessop Avenue, Cheltenham GL50 3SH. Publishes a guide to PGCE courses.

Historical Association – 59a Kennington Park Road, London SE11 4JH. Tel: 0171 735 3901.

Institute of Personnel and Development – IPD House, Camp Road, London SW19 4UX. Tel: 0181 946 9100.

London Montessori Centre – 18 Balderton Street, London W1Y 1TG. Tel: 0171 493 0165.

Maria Montessori Training Organisation – 26 Lyndhurst Gardens, London NW3 5NW. Tel: 0171 435 3646.

National Academic Recognition Centre (NARIC) – at the British Council, Medlock Street, Manchester M15 4AA.

National Society for Education in Art and Design – The Gatehouse, Corsham Court, Corsham, Wiltshire SN13 0BZ. Tel: 01249 714825.

Physical Education Association of the United Kingdom (PEA UK) – Suite 5–10, Churchill Square, West Malling, Kent ME19 4DU. Tel: 01732 875888. Can supply careers information on receipt of a stamped addressed envelope. Also produce a brochure *A Career in Physical Education, Sport and Recreation.*

Pre-School Learning Alliance – 61–63, Kings Cross Road, London WC1X 9LL. Tel: 0171 833 0991.

Professional Council for Religious Education – Royal Buildings, Victoria Street, Derby DE1 1GW Tel: 01332 296655 – publishes a leaflet on the career possibilities of religious studies.

Royal Geographical Society – 1 Kensington Gore, London SW7 2AR. Tel: 0171 589 5466.

Teacher Education Admission Clearing House (TEACH) – PO Box 165, Edinburgh EH8 8AT – for information on teaching in Scotland.

Teacher Training Agency – Communication Centre, PO Box 3210, Chelmsford, Essex CM1 3WA. Tel: 01245 454454. Contact for information on teaching and teacher training.

Careers in Teaching, published by Kogan Page.

Careers Working with Children and Young People, published by Kogan Page.

Guide to Courses and Careers in Art, Craft and Design, by Tony Charlton, available from the National Society for Education in Art and Design (address above).

Handbook of Initial Teacher Training, published annually by NATFHE – the directory of teacher training courses.

Music Teachers' Yearbook, available from Rhinegold Publishing.

Teaching in Schools and Colleges in the UK, AGCAS Occupational Series booklet, available from CSU, Crawford House, Precinct Centre, Manchester M13 9EP.

Using Languages, AGCAS Special Interest Series for graduates (see above address).

Working in Languages, published by COIC (Sales Department, Room E414, Moorfoot, Sheffield S1 4PQ).

Working in Teaching, published by COIC.

Working in Work with Children, published by COIC.

See the *Times Educational Supplement* (Fridays) for an idea of vacancies and the sorts of issues which are of concern to educationists.

TEACHING – SPECIAL NEEDS

Committee for Steiner Special Education – c/o Philpotts Manor School, West Hoathly, West Sussex RH19 4PR. Tel: 01342 810268.

The Shaftesbury Society – 16–20 Kingston Rd, South Wimbledon, London SW19 1JZ. Tel: 0181 542 5550 – for general information on schools run by the society.

TEACHING OVERSEAS AND TEFL

ARELS Ltd (Association of Recognised English Language Schools) – 2 Pontypool Place, Valentine Place, London SE1 8QP. Tel: 0171 242 3136/7.

BASCELT – (British Association of State Colleges in English Language Teaching), Francis Close Hall, Swindon Road, Cheltenham, Gloucester GL50 4AZ. Tel: 01242 227099. Produces an annual guide to courses in the state sector.

British Council – Overseas Appointments Services, Medlock Street, Manchester M15 4AA. Tel: 0161 957 7383.

British Council (English Language Information Unit) – 10 Spring Gardens, London SW1A 2BN. The British Council English Language Information Section produces information sheets on entering TEFL/TESL teaching, and publishes *TEFL/TESL Academic Courses in the UK*.

Central Bureau for Educational Visits and Exchanges – 10 Spring Gardens, London SW1A 2BN. Tel: 0171 389 4004.

English Speaking Board – 26a Prince's Street, Southport, Merseyside PR8 1EQ. Tel: 01704 501730.

European Council of International Schools – 21 Lavant Street, Petersfield, Hampshire GU32 3EL. Tel: 01730 268244.

Gabbitas Educational Consultants Ltd – Carrington House, 126–130 Regent Street, London W1R 6EE. Tel: 0171 734 0161.

Overseas Development Administration – Abercrombie House, Eaglesham Road, East Kilbride, Glasgow G75 8EA. Tel: 01355 843167.

RSA/UCLES – Syndicate Buildings, 1 Hills Road, Cambridge CB1 2EU. Tel: 01223 553311.

Trinity College – 16 Park Crescent, London W1M 4AH. Tel: 0171 323 2328.

Voluntary Service Overseas – 317 Putney Bridge Road, London SW15 2PN. Tel: 0181 780 2266.

World Service Enquiry – Christians Abroad, 1 Stockwell Green, London SW9 9HP. Tel: 0171 737 7811.

Teaching English Abroad, by Susan Griffith, published by Vacation Work.

Teaching English as a Foreign Language and Teaching Abroad, AGCAS Occupational Series, available from Central Services Unit, Crawford House, Oxford Road, Manchester M13 9EP.

Teaching English in the EU, published by Careers Europe, 4th Floor, Midland House, 14 Cheapside, Bradford BD1 4JA.

For job advertisements see the *Times Educational Supplement* (Fridays), the *Guardian* (Tuesday edition), and *Overseas Jobs Express* – published fortnightly and available on subscription from Premier House, Shoreham Airport, Sussex BN43 5FF.

Vacancies are also advertised in the *EFL Gazette* (monthly from 10 Wrights Lane, Kensington, London W8 6TA).

For courses in the private sector, a guide can be obtained from ARELS Ltd (address above).